Peter Stull
Bath 8 AM
Cori
Eat Out 5 PM
BK

PRAYERS OF ECSTASY!

PRAYERS OF ECSTASY

SELECTIONS FROM
THE BAHÁ'Í SACRED WRITINGS
Large Type Edition

> *Let your joy*
> *be the joy*
> *born of My Most Great Name,*
> *a Name that bringeth rapture*
> *to the heart,*
> *and filleth with ecstasy*
> *the minds*
> *of all who have*
> *drawn nigh unto God.*
> —Bahá'u'lláh

KALIMÁT PRESS • LOS ANGELES

Copyright © 2001 by Kalimát Press
All Rights Reserved
Manufactured in the United States of America
Large Type Edition

Library of Congress Cataloging-in-Publication Data

Prayers of ecstasy: selections from the Bahá'í sacred writings.
p.cm.
ISBN 1-890688-13-4
1. Bahai Faith—Prayer-books and devotions—English.
I. Kalimat Press.

BP380 .P74 2001
297.9'3433—dc21   2001029484

Cover and book design by Judith Wright Liggett

Kalimát Press
1600 Sawtelle Boulevard, Suite 310
Los Angeles, California 90025

www.kalimat.com / kalimatp@aol.com

CONTENTS

The headings designated below are purely arbitrary, for the purpose of easier location of the prayers. They form no part of the Sacred Text itself.

Proclaiming the Kingdom

He Is Come! 3
Glad-Tidings! 8
The Path to the Kingdom 13

Prayers and Passages

Praise! 21
Love! 31
Fire 36
Intoxication 44
Rapture! 52
Ecstasy! 56
Sorrow and Joy 60
Seeking 68
Gathering 75

Meditations

Alláh-u Abhá!   83
Tablet of Aḥmad   85
Long Healing Prayer   90
Fire Tablet   99
Tablet of the Holy Mariner   107
Tablet of the True Seeker   117
Perspicuous Verses   127
The Blessings   133

*Reveal then Thyself, O Lord,
by Thy merciful utterance
and the mystery of Thy divine being,
that the holy ecstasy of prayer
may fill our souls—
a prayer that shall rise above
words and letters
and transcend the murmur
of syllables and sounds—
that all things may be merged
into nothingness
before the revelation of Thy splendor.*

—'Abdu'l-Bahá

'Abdu'l-Bahá

Proclaiming the Kingdom

Verily, verily,
the new heaven and the new earth are come.
The holy City, new Jerusalem,
hath come down from on high . . .
He hath wiped away their tears,
kindled their light,
rejoiced their hearts
and enraptured their souls.
Death shall no more overtake them
neither shall sorrow,
weeping or tribulation afflict them.
The Lord God Omnipotent
hath been enthroned in His Kingdom
and hath made all things new.

– 'Abdu'l-Bahá

He Is Come!

Proclaim unto every longing lover: "Behold, your Well-Beloved hath come among men!"
—Bahá'u'lláh

O thou who art waiting, tarry no longer, for He is come. Behold His Tabernacle and His Glory dwelling therein. It is the Ancient Glory, with a new Manifestation.

— *Bahá'u'lláh*

The time foreordained unto the peoples and kindreds of the earth is now come. The promises of God, as recorded in the holy Scriptures, have all been fulfilled. Out of Zion hath gone forth the Law of God, and Jerusalem, and the hills and land thereof, are filled with the glory of His Revelation. Happy is the man that pondereth in his heart that which hath been revealed in the Books of God, the Help in Peril, the Self-Subsisting.

Meditate upon this, O ye beloved of God, and let your ears be attentive unto His Word, so that ye may, by His grace and mercy, drink your fill from the crystal waters of constancy, and become as steadfast and immovable as the mountain in His Cause.

— *Bahá'u'lláh*

⁂

Call out to Zion, O Carmel, and announce the joyful tidings: He that was hidden from mortal eyes is come! His all-conquering sovereignty is manifest; His all-encompassing splendor is revealed.

Beware lest thou hesitate or halt. Hasten forth and circumambulate the City of God that

hath descended from heaven, the celestial Kaaba round which have circled in adoration the favored of God, the pure in heart, and the company of the most exalted angels.
— *Bahá'u'lláh*

O peoples of the world! The Sun of Truth hath risen to illumine the whole earth, and to spiritualize the community of man. Laudable are the results and the fruits thereof, abundant the holy evidences deriving from this grace. This is mercy unalloyed and purest bounty; it is light for the world and all its peoples; it is harmony and fellowship, and love and solidarity; indeed it is compassion and unity, and the end of foreignness; it is the being at one, in complete dignity and freedom, with all on earth.

The Blessed Beauty saith: "Ye are all the fruits of one tree, the leaves of one branch." Thus hath He likened this world of being to a single tree, and all its peoples to the leaves thereof, and the blossoms and fruits. It is needful for the bough to blossom, and leaf and fruit to flourish, and upon the interconnection of all parts of the world-tree, dependeth the flourishing of leaf and blossom, and the sweetness of the fruit.

For this reason must all human beings powerfully sustain one another and seek for everlasting life; and for this reason must the lovers of God in this contingent world become the mercies and the blessings sent forth by that clement King of the seen and unseen realms. Let them purify their sight and behold all humankind as leaves and blossoms and fruits of the tree of being. Let them at all times concern themselves with doing a kindly thing for one of their fellows, offering to someone love, consideration, thoughtful help. Let them see no one as their enemy, or as wishing them ill, but think of all humankind as their friends; regarding the alien as an intimate, the stranger as a companion, staying free of prejudice, drawing no lines.

In this day, the one favored at the Threshold of the Lord is he who handeth round the cup of faithfulness; who bestoweth, even upon his enemies, the jewel of bounty, and lendeth, even to his fallen oppressor, a helping hand; it is he who will, even to the fiercest of his foes, be a loving friend. These are the Teachings of the Blessed Beauty, these the counsels of the Most Great Name.

—*'Abdu'l-Bahá*

Glad Tidings!

Glad Tidings! Glad Tidings!
The Morn of Guidance hath dawned.
Glad Tidings! Glad Tidings!
The Sun of Reality hath shone forth.
Glad Tidings! Glad Tidings!
The Breeze of Favor hath wafted.
Glad Tidings! Glad Tidings!
The raindrops of the Cloud of Bounty have showered.
Glad Tidings! Glad Tidings!
The Sun of the Supreme Horizon hath radiated to all the world with boundless Effulgence.
Glad Tidings! Glad Tidings!
The hearts are all in the utmost purity.

Glad Tidings! Glad Tidings!
It is the splendor of His Holiness Bahá.
Glad Tidings! Glad Tidings!
Zion is dancing.
Glad Tidings! Glad Tidings!
The Kingdom of God is full of Exhilaration and Commotion.

—*'Abdu'l-Bahá*

The Sun of Reality hath appeared and flooded all regions with its glorious light; it has upraised the Standard of Oneness of the world of humanity and summoned all mankind to the refulgent Truth. The cloud of Mercy is pouring, the zephyr of Providence is wafting and the world of humanity is being stirred and moved. The Divine Spirit is conferring eternal life, the heavenly lights are illumining the hearts, the table of the sustenance of the Kingdom is spread and adorned with all kinds of foods and victuals.

O ye concourses of men! Awake! Awake! Become mindful! Become mindful! Open ye the seeing eye! Unstop the hearing ear! Hark! Hark!

The soft notes of the Heavenly Music are streaming down, ravishing the ears of the people of spiritual discernment. Ere long this transcendent Light will wholly enlighten the East and West!

—'Abdu'l-Bahá

O ye friends of God!
Do ye know in what cycle ye are created and in what age ye exist? This is the age of the Blessed Perfection and this is the time of the Greatest Name! This is the century of the Manifestation, the age of the Sun of the horizons and the beautiful springtime of the Eternal One!

The earth is in motion and growth; the mountains, hills and prairies are green and pleasant; the bounty is overflowing; mercy universal; the rain is descending from the cloud of compassion; the brilliant sun is shining; the full moon adorneth the ethereal horizon; the great ocean-tide is flooding every little stream; the gifts and favors follow one upon the other and a refreshing breeze is blowing, wafting the fragrant perfume of the blossoms.

If we are not happy and joyous at this season, for what other season shall we wait and for what other time shall we look?

Boundless treasure is in the hand of the King of Kings! Lift the hem of thy garment in order to receive it.

This is the time for growing; the season for joyous gathering! Take the cup of the Testament in thy hand; leap and dance with ecstasy in the triumphal procession of the Covenant! Place your confidence in the everlasting bounty, turn to the presence of the generous God; ask assistance from the Kingdom of Abhá; seek confirmation from the Supreme World; turn thy vision to the horizon of eternal wealth; and pray for help from the Source of Mercy!

—*'Abdu'l-Bahá*

The Path to the Kingdom

The first thing to do is to acquire a thirst for Spirituality, then Live the Life! Live the Life! Live the Life!

—'Abdu'l-Bahá

Worlds, holy and spiritually glorious, will be unveiled to your eyes.

—Bahá'u'lláh

Those souls that, in this day, enter the divine kingdom and attain everlasting life, although materially dwelling on earth, yet in reality soar in the realm of heaven. Their bodies may linger on earth but their spirits travel in the immensity of space. For as thoughts widen and become illumined, they acquire the power of flight and transport man to the kingdom of God.

—'Abdu'l-Bahá

❦

The world of the Kingdom is sanctified from everything that can be perceived by the eye or by the other senses—hearing, smell, taste or touch. The mind which is in man, the existence of which is recognized—where is it in him? If you examine the body . . . you will not find it; nevertheless, it exists. Therefore, the mind has no place, but it is connected with the brain.

The Kingdom is also like this. In the same way love has no place, but it is connected with the heart; so the Kingdom has no place, but is connected with man.

Entrance into the Kingdom is through the love of God, through detachment, through holiness and chastity, through truthfulness, purity, steadfastness, faithfulness and the sacrifice of life.

—'Abdu'l-Bahá

༄

If he attains rebirth while in the world of nature, he will become informed of the divine world. He will observe that another and a higher world exists. Wonderful bounties descend; eternal life awaits; everlasting glory surrounds him. All the signs of reality and greatness are there. He will see the lights of God.

—'Abdu'l-Bahá

༄

Although the Kingdom of heaven is hidden from the sight of this unwitting people, still, to him who seeth with the inner eye, it is plain as day.

Wherefore dwell thou ever in the Kingdom, and be thou oblivious of the world below. Be thou so wholly absorbed in the emanations of the spirit that nothing in the world of man will distract thee.

—'Abdu'l-Bahá

⁂

To every human being must ye be infinitely kind. Call none a stranger; think none to be your foe. Be ye as if all men were your close kin and honored friends. Walk ye in such wise that this fleeting world will change into a splendor and this dismal heap of dust become a palace of delights.

—'Abdu'l-Bahá

⁂

Know, verily, that the Ocean is waving, the Sun is shining, the Stars dawning. (Understand what I say!) The tree will grow, the earth will send forth hyacinths and give blessings, and man will become of the heavenly angels. Feed on the light of guidance and impart light to the people. The bird will warble melodies unknown save by the birds of heaven; then tear asunder the veil and see the realities of things with the eye of God.

—'Abdu'l-Bahá

Prayers and Passages

> . . . in this garden of God,
> lift up your voices
> and sing the blissful anthems
> of the spirit.
> Become ye as the birds
> who offer Him their thanks,
> and in the blossoming bowers of life,
> chant ye such melodies,
> as will dazzle the minds
> of those who know.
>
> —'Abdu'l-Bahá

PRAISE!

That which the people possess, and the treasures of the earth, and that which the rulers and kings own, are not equal in this day to the singing of His praise.
—Bahá'u'lláh

Praise be unto Thee, Who art my God and the God of all men, and my Desire and the Desire of all them that have recognized Thee, and my Beloved and the Beloved of such as have acknowledged Thy unity, and the Object of my adoration and of the adoration of them that have near access to Thee, and my Wish and the Wish of such as are wholly devoted to Thee, and my Hope and the Hope of them that have fixed their hearts upon Thee, and my Refuge and the Refuge of all such as have hastened towards Thee, and my Haven and the Haven of whosoever hath repaired unto Thee, and my Goal and the Goal of all them that have set themselves towards Thee, and my Object and the Object of those who have fixed their gaze upon Thee, and my Paradise and the Paradise of them that have ascended towards Thee, and my Lode-star and the Lode-star of all such as yearn after Thee, and my Joy and the Joy of all them that love Thee, and my Light and the Light of all such as have erred and asked to be forgiven by Thee, and my Exultation and the Exultation of all them that remember Thee, and my Stronghold and the Stronghold of all such as have fled to Thee, and my Sanctuary and the Sanctuary of all that dread Thee, and my Lord and the Lord of all such as dwell in the heavens and on the earth!

—Bahá'u'lláh

Praise be to Thee, O my God, that Thou hast revealed Thy favors and Thy bounties; and glory be to Thee, O my Beloved, that Thou hast manifested the Day-Star of Thy loving-kindness and Thy tender mercies.

I yield Thee such thanks as can direct the steps of the wayward towards the splendors of the morning light of Thy guidance, and enable those who yearn towards Thee to attain the seat of the revelation of the effulgence of Thy beauty.

I yield Thee such thanks as can cause the sick to draw nigh unto the waters of Thy healing, and can help those who are far from Thee to approach the living fountain of Thy presence.

I yield Thee such thanks as can divest the bodies of Thy servants of the garments of mortality and abasement, and attire them in the robes of Thine eternity and Thy glory, and lead the poor unto the shores of Thy holiness and all sufficient riches.

I yield Thee such thanks as can enable the Heavenly Dove to warble forth, upon the branches of the Lote-Tree of Immortality, her song: "Verily, Thou art God. No God is there besides Thee. From eternity Thou hast been exalted above the praise of aught else but Thee, and been high above the description of any one except Thyself."

I yield Thee such thanks as can cause the Nightingale of Glory to pour forth its melody in the highest heaven: " 'Alí,* in truth, is Thy servant, Whom Thou hast singled out from among Thy Messengers and Thy chosen Ones, and made Him to be the Manifestation of Thyself in all that pertaineth unto Thee, and that concerneth the revelation of Thine attributes and the evidences of Thy names."

I yield Thee such thanks as can stir up all things to extol Thee, and to glorify Thine Essence, and can unloose the tongues of all beings to magnify the sovereignty of Thy beauty.

*The Báb.

I yield Thee such thanks as can fill the heavens and the earth with the signs of Thy transcendent Essence, and assist all created things to enter the Tabernacle of Thy nearness and Thy presence.

I yield Thee such thanks as can make every created thing to be a book that shall speak of Thee, and a scroll that shall unfold Thy praise.

I yield Thee such thanks as can establish the Manifestations of Thy sovereignty upon the throne of Thy governance, and set up the Exponents of Thy glory upon the seat of Thy Divinity.

I yield Thee such thanks as can make the corrupt tree to bring forth good fruit through the holy breaths of Thy favors, and revive the bodies of all beings with the gentle winds of Thy transcendent grace.

I yield Thee such thanks as can cause the signs of Thine exalted singleness to be sent down out of the heaven of Thy holy unity.

I yield Thee such thanks as can teach all things the realities of Thy knowledge and the essence of Thy wisdom, and will not withhold the wretched creatures from the doors of Thy mercy and Thy bountiful favor.

I yield Thee such thanks as can enable all who are in heaven and on earth to dispense with all created things, through the treasuries of Thine all-sufficing riches, and can aid all created things to reach unto the summit of Thine almighty favors.

I yield Thee such thanks as can assist the hearts of Thine ardent lovers to soar into the atmosphere of nearness to Thee, and of longing for Thee, and kindle the Light of Lights within the land of Iraq.

I yield Thee such thanks as can detach them that are nigh unto Thee from all created things, and draw them to the throne of Thy names and Thine attributes.

I yield Thee such thanks as can cause Thee to forgive all sins and trespasses, and to fulfill the needs of the peoples of all religions, and to waft the fragrances of pardon over the entire creation.

I yield Thee such thanks as can enable

them that recognize Thy unity to scale the heights of Thy love, and cause such as are devoted to Thee to ascend unto the Paradise of Thy presence.

I yield Thee such thanks as can satisfy the wants of all such as seek Thee, and realize the aims of them that have recognized Thee.

I yield Thee such thanks as can blot out from the hearts of men all suggestions of limitations, and inscribe the signs of Thy unity.

I yield Thee such thanks as that with which Thou didst from eternity glorify Thine own Self, and didst exalt it above all peers, rivals, and comparisons, O Thou in Whose hands are the heavens of grace and of bounty, and the kingdoms of glory and of majesty!

—Bahá'u'lláh

My God, my Adored One, my King, my Desire!

What tongue can voice my thanks to Thee?

I was heedless, Thou didst awaken me. I had turned back from Thee, Thou didst graciously aid me to turn towards Thee. I was as one dead, Thou didst quicken me with the water of life. I was withered, Thou didst revive me with the heavenly stream of Thine utterance which hath flowed forth from the Pen of the All-Merciful.

O Divine Providence! All existence is begotten by Thy bounty; deprive it not of the waters of Thy generosity, neither do Thou withhold it from the ocean of Thy mercy. I beseech Thee to aid and assist me at all times and under all conditions, and seek from the heaven of Thy grace Thine ancient favor. Thou art, in truth, the Lord of bounty, and the Sovereign of the kingdom of eternity.

—*Bahá'u'lláh*

O compassionate God! Thanks be to Thee for Thou hast awakened and made me conscious. Thou hast given me a seeing eye and favored me with a hearing ear, hast led me to Thy kingdom and guided me to Thy path. Thou hast shown me the right way and caused me to enter the ark of deliverance.

O God! Keep me steadfast and make me firm and staunch. Protect me from violent tests, and preserve and shelter me in the strongly fortified fortress of Thy Covenant and Testament. Thou art the Powerful. Thou art the Seeing. Thou art the Hearing.

O Thou the Compassionate God. Bestow upon me a heart which, like unto a glass, may be illumined with the light of Thy love, and confer upon me thoughts which may change this world into a rose garden through the outpourings of heavenly grace.

Thou art the Compassionate, the Merciful. Thou art the Great Beneficent God.

—'Abdu'l-Bahá

Praise be to God!
His Traces are evident.
Praise be to God!
His Lights are radiating.
Praise be to God!
His Ocean is full of waves.
Praise be to God!
His Radiance is intense.
Praise be to God!
His Bestowals are abundant.
Praise be to God!
His Favors are manifest.

—'Abdu'l-Bahá

LOVE!

Until love takes possession of the heart, no other divine bounty can be revealed in it.
—'Abdu'l-Bahá

Praise be to Thee, O Lord my God! I implore Thee, by Thy Name which none hath befittingly recognized, and whose import no soul hath fathomed; I beseech Thee, by Him Who is the Fountain-Head of Thy Revelation and the Day-Spring of Thy signs, to make my heart to be a receptacle of Thy love and of remembrance of Thee. Knit it, then, to Thy most great Ocean, that from it may flow out the living waters of Thy wisdom and the crystal streams of Thy glorification and praise.
—Bahá'u'lláh

In the love I bear to Thee, O my Lord, my heart longeth for Thee with a longing such as no heart hath known. Here am I with my body between Thy hands, and my spirit before Thy face. Do with them as it may please Thee, for the exaltation of Thy word, and the revelation of what hath been enshrined within the treasuries of Thy knowledge.

Potent art Thou to do what Thou willest, and able to ordain what Thou pleasest.

—*Bahá'u'lláh*

I am well aware, O my Lord, that I have been so carried away by the clear tokens of Thy loving-kindness, and so completely inebriated with the wine of Thine utterance, that whatever I behold I readily discover that it maketh Thee known unto me, and it remindeth me of Thy signs, and of Thy tokens, and of Thy testimonies.

By Thy glory! Every time I lift up mine eyes unto Thy heaven, I call to mind Thy highness and Thy loftiness, and Thine incomparable glory and greatness; and every time I turn my gaze to Thine earth, I am made to recognize the evidences of Thy power and the tokens of Thy bounty. And when I behold the sea, I find that it speaketh to me of Thy majesty, and of the potency of Thy might, and of Thy sovereignty and Thy grandeur. And at whatever time I contemplate the mountains, I am led to discover the ensigns of Thy victory and the standards of Thine omnipotence.

I swear by Thy might, O Thou in Whose grasp are the reins of all mankind, and the destinies of the nations! I am so inflamed by my love for Thee, and so inebriated with the wine of Thy oneness, that I can hear from the whisper of the winds the sound of Thy glorification and praise, and can recognize in the murmur of the waters the voice that proclaimeth Thy virtues and Thine attributes, and can apprehend from the rustling of the leaves the mysteries that have been irrevocably ordained by Thee in Thy realm.

Glorified art Thou, O God of all names and Creator of the heavens!

—Bahá'u'lláh

○○○

O my God! O my God! Glory be unto Thee for that Thou hast confirmed me to the confession of Thy oneness, attracted me unto the word of Thy singleness, enkindled me by the fire of Thy love, and occupied me with Thy mention and the service of Thy friends and maidservants.

O Lord, help me to be meek and lowly, and strengthen me in severing myself from all things and in holding to the hem of the garment of Thy glory, so that my heart may be filled with Thy love and leave no space for love of the world and attachment to its qualities.

O God! Sanctify me from all else save Thee, purge me from the dross of sins and transgressions, and cause me to possess a spiritual heart and conscience.

Verily, Thou art merciful and, verily, Thou art the Most Generous, Whose help is sought by all men.

—'Abdu'l-Bahá

Fire

*O God, create in the hearts of Thy beloved
the fire of Thy love . . .*
—Bahá'u'lláh

All praise be to Thee, O Lord, my God! How mysterious the Fire which Thou hast enkindled within my heart! My very limbs testify to the intensity of its heat, and evince the consuming power of its flame. Should my bodily tongue ever attempt to describe Thee as the One Whose strength hath ever excelled the strength of the most mighty amongst men, the tongue of my heart would address me, saying: "These are but words which can only be adequate to such things as are of the same likeness and nature as themselves. But He, of a truth, is infinitely exalted above the mention of all His creatures."

The power of Thy might beareth me witness, O my Well-Beloved! Every limb of my body, methinks, is endowed with a tongue that glorifieth Thee and magnifieth Thy name. Armed with the power of Thy love, the hatred which moveth them that are against Thee can never alarm me; and with Thy praise on my lips, the rulings of Thy decree can in no wise fill me with sorrow. Fortify, therefore, Thy love within my breast, and suffer me to face the assaults which all the peoples of the earth may launch against me. I swear by Thee! Every hair of my head proclaimeth: "But for the adversities that befall me in Thy path, how could I ever taste the divine sweetness of Thy tenderness and love?"

Send down, therefore, O my Lord, upon me and upon them that love me, that which will cause us to become steadfast in Thy Faith. Enable them, then, to become the Hands of Thy Cause amongst Thy servants, that they may scatter abroad Thy signs, and show forth Thy sovereignty. There is no God but Thee, Who art powerful to do whatsoever Thou willest. Thou art, in truth, the All-Glorious, the All-Praised.

—Bahá'u'lláh

I know not, O my God, what the Fire is which Thou didst kindle in Thy land. Earth can never cloud its splendor, nor water quench its flame. All the peoples of the world are powerless to resist its force. Great is the blessedness of him that hath drawn nigh unto it, and heard its roaring.

Some, O my God, Thou didst, through Thy strengthening grace, enable to approach it, while others Thou didst keep back by reason of what their hands have wrought in Thy days. Whoso hath hasted towards it and attained unto it hath, in his eagerness to gaze on Thy beauty, yielded his life in Thy path, and ascended unto Thee, wholly detached from aught else except Thyself.

I beseech Thee, O my Lord, by this Fire which blazeth and rageth in the world of creation, to rend asunder the veils that have hindered me from appearing before the throne of Thy majesty, and from standing at the door of Thy gate. Do Thou ordain for me, O my Lord, every good thing Thou didst send down in Thy Book, and suffer me not to be far removed from the shelter of Thy mercy.

Powerful art Thou to do what pleaseth Thee. Thou art, verily, the All-Powerful, the Most Generous.

—Bahá'u'lláh

Behold Thou this stranger, O my Lord, who hath hastened to attain his most exalted Home in the shelter of Thy shadowing mercy, and this ailing soul who hath set his face towards the ocean of Thy healing.

Look, then, O Thou my God Who settest my soul on fire, upon the tears I shed, and the sighs I utter, and the anguish that afflicteth my heart and the fire that consumeth my being. Thy glory beareth me witness, O Thou, the Light of the world! The fire of Thy love that burneth continually within me hath so inflamed me that whoever among Thy creatures approacheth me, and inclineth his inner ear towards me, cannot fail to hear its raging within each of my veins.

I am so carried away by the sweetness of Thine utterances, and so inebriated with the wine of Thy tender mercies, that my voice can never be stilled, nor can my suppliant hands any longer desist from being stretched out towards Thee.

Thou seest, O my Lord, how mine eyes are fixed in the direction of Thy grace, and mine ears inclined towards the kingdom of Thine utterance, and my tongue unloosed to celebrate Thy praise, and my face set towards Thy face that surviveth all that hath been created by

Thy word, and my hands raised up towards the heaven of Thy bounty and favor.
—Bahá'u'lláh

Magnified, O Lord my God, be Thy Name, whereby the trees of the garden of Thy Revelation have been clad with verdure, and been made to yield the fruits of holiness during this Springtime when the sweet savors of Thy favors and blessings have been wafted over all things, and caused them to bring forth whatsoever had been preordained for them in the Kingdom of Thine irrevocable decree and the Heaven of Thine immutable purpose. I beseech Thee by this very Name not to suffer me to be far from the court of Thy holiness, nor debarred from the exalted sanctuary of Thy unity and oneness.

Ignite, then, O my God, within my breast the fire of Thy love, that its flame may burn up all else except my remembrance of Thee, that every trace of corrupt desire may be entirely mortified within me, and that naught may remain except the glorification of Thy transcendent and all-glorious Being. This is my highest aspiration, mine ardent desire, O Thou Who rulest all things, and in Whose hand is the kingdom of the entire creation. Thou, verily, doest what Thou choosest. No God is there beside Thee, the Almighty, the All-Glorious, the Ever-Forgiving.

—*Bahá'u'lláh*

O my God! O my God! I am a servant attracted to Thee, humbly drawing near to the door of Thy Oneness, and supplicating the Kingdom of Thy mercy.

O my God, permit me to be entirely Thine, occupied only with thoughts of Thee, inflamed by the fire of Thy love and separated from all except Thee, so that I may work in Thy Cause, spread Thy wisdom, transmit Thy knowledge and impart the joy of knowing Thee.

O my God, I am a flame lighted by the hands of Thy power; let not that flame be quenched by the winds of trials. Increase my love for Thee, my ardor for the beauty of Thy Oneness. Kindle the fire that burns in me in the Sinai of Thy Singleness, and awaken the eternal life that is latent in me, through Thy bounty and grace.

Thou art the Protector, the Watcher, the Compassionate and the Merciful.

—'Abdu'l-Bahá

INTOXICATION

All wine hath depression as an after-effect, except the wine of the Love of God.
—'Abdu'l-Bahá

Think not that the wine We have mentioned in Our Tablets is the wine which men drink, and which causeth their intelligence to pass away, their human nature to be perverted, their light to be changed, and their purity to be soiled. Our intention is indeed that wine which intensifieth man's love for God, for His Chosen Ones and for His loved ones, and igniteth in the hearts the fire of God and love for Him, and glorification and praise of Him.

So potent is this wine that a drop thereof

will attract him who drinketh it to the court of His sanctity and nearness, and will enable him to attain the presence of God, the King, the Glorious, the Most Beauteous. It is a wine that blotteth out from the hearts of the true lovers all suggestions of limitation, establisheth the truth of the signs of His oneness and divine unity, and leadeth them to the Tabernacle of the Well-Beloved, in the presence of God, the Sovereign Lord, the Self-Subsisting, the All-Forgiving, the All-Generous.

We meant by this Wine, the River of God, and His favor, the fountain of His living waters, and the Mystic Wine and its divine grace, even as it was revealed in the Qur'an, if ye are of those who understand. He said, and how true is His utterance: "A wine delectable to those who drink it."* And He had no purpose in this but the wine we have mentioned to you, O people of certitude!

—*Bahá'u'lláh*

*Qu'ran 47:15.

To all that dwell on earth I cry aloud and say: "Fear ye God, O ye servants of God, and suffer not yourselves to be kept back from this pure Wine that hath flowed from the right hand of the throne of the mercy of your Lord, the Most Merciful. I swear by God! Better for you is what He possesseth than the things ye yourselves possess and the things ye have sought and are now seeking in this vain and empty life. Forsake the world, and set your faces towards the all-glorious Horizon. Whoso hath partaken of the wine of His remembrance will forget every other remembrance, and whoso hath recognized Him will rid himself of all attachment to this life and to all that pertaineth unto it."

I implore Thee, O my God and my Master, by Thy word through which they who have believed in Thy unity have soared up into the atmosphere of Thy knowledge, and they who are devoted to Thee have ascended into the heaven of Thy oneness, to inspire Thy loved ones with that which will assure their hearts in

Thy Cause. Endue them with such steadfastness that nothing whatsoever will hinder them from turning towards Thee.

Thou art, verily, the Bountiful, the Munificent, the Forgiving, the Compassionate.
—*Bahá'u'lláh*

⁓✵⁓

I beseech Thee by Thy Name through which Thou hast revealed Thy Self, in the glory of Thy most excellent titles, unto all created things, in this Revelation whereby Thou hast, through Thy most resplendent Name, manifested Thy beauty, to give me to drink of the wine of Thy mercy and of the pure beverage of Thy favor, which have streamed forth from the right hand of Thy will, that I may so fix my gaze upon Thee and be so detached from all else but Thee, that the world and all that hath been created therein may appear before me as a fleeting day which Thou hast not deigned to create.

I moreover entreat Thee, O my God, to

rain down, from the heaven of Thy will and the clouds of Thy mercy, that which will cleanse us from the noisome savors of our transgressions, O Thou Who hast called Thyself the God of Mercy! Thou art, verily, the Most Powerful, the All-Glorious, the Beneficent.

Cast not away, O my Lord, him that hath turned towards Thee, nor suffer him who hath drawn nigh unto Thee to be removed far from Thy court. Dash not the hopes of the suppliant who hath longingly stretched out his hands to seek Thy grace and favors, and deprive not Thy sincere servants of the wonders of Thy tender mercies and loving-kindness. Forgiving and Most Bountiful art Thou, O my Lord! Power hast Thou to do what Thou pleasest. All else but Thee are impotent before the revelations of Thy might, are as lost in the face of the evidences of Thy wealth, are as nothing when compared with the manifestations of Thy transcendent sovereignty, and are destitute of all strength when face to face with the signs and tokens of Thy power.

What refuge is there beside Thee, O my

Lord, to which I can flee, and where is there a haven to which I can hasten? Nay, the power of Thy might beareth me witness! No protector is there but Thee, no place to flee to except Thee, no refuge to seek save Thee. Cause me to taste, O my Lord, the divine sweetness of Thy remembrance and praise. I swear by Thy might! Whosoever tasteth of its sweetness will rid himself of all attachment to the world and all that is therein, and will set his face towards Thee, cleansed from the remembrance of any one except Thee.

Inspire then my soul, O my God, with Thy wondrous remembrance, that I may glorify Thy name. Number me not with them who read Thy words and fail to find Thy hidden gift which, as decreed by Thee, is contained therein, and which quickeneth the souls of Thy creatures and the hearts of Thy servants. Cause me, O my Lord, to be reckoned among them who have been so stirred up by the sweet savors that have been wafted in Thy days that they have laid down their lives for Thee and hastened to the scene of their death in their long-

ing to gaze on Thy beauty and in their yearning to attain Thy presence. And were any one to say unto them on their way, "Whither go ye?" they would say, "Unto God, the All-Possessing, the Help in Peril, the Self-Subsisting!"
—*Bahá'u'lláh*

O my God! O my God!
This, Thy servant, hath advanced towards Thee, is passionately wandering in the desert of Thy love, walking in the path of Thy service, anticipating Thy favors, hoping for Thy bounty, relying upon Thy kingdom, and intoxicated by the wine of Thy gift. O my God! Increase the fervor of his affection for Thee, the constancy of his praise of Thee, and the ardor of his love for Thee.

Verily, Thou art the Most Generous, the Lord of grace abounding. There is no other God but Thee, the Forgiving, the Merciful.
—*'Abdu'l-Bahá*

O Divine Providence!
Bestow Thou in all things purity and cleanliness upon the people of Bahá. Grant that they be freed from all defilement, and released from all addictions. Save them from committing any repugnant act, unbind them from the chains of every evil habit, that they may live pure and free, wholesome and cleanly, worthy to serve at Thy Sacred Threshold and fit to be related to their Lord.

Deliver them from intoxicating drinks and tobacco, save them, rescue them, from this opium that bringeth on madness, suffer them to enjoy the sweet savors of holiness, that they may drink deep of the mystic cup of heavenly love and know the rapture of being drawn ever closer unto the Realm of the All-Glorious. For it is even as Thou hast said: "All that thou hast in thy cellar will not appease the thirst of my love—bring me, O cup-bearer, of the wine of the spirit a cup as full as the sea!"

—'Abdu'l-Bahá

RAPTURE!

Whoever hath been transported by the rapture born of adoration for My Name, the Most Compassionate, will recite the verses of God in such wise as to captivate the hearts of those yet wrapped in slumber.
— Bahá'u'lláh

O Thou the Lord of the visible and the invisible, and the Enlightener of all creation!

I beseech Thee, by Thy sovereignty which is hid from the eyes of men, to reveal in all directions the signs of Thy manifold blessings and the tokens of Thy loving-kindness, that I may arise with exultation and rapture and extol Thy wondrous virtues, O Thou the Most Merciful, and stir up by Thy name all created

things, and so kindle the fire of Thy glorification amidst Thy creatures, that all the world may be filled with the brightness of the light of Thy glory, and all existence be inflamed with the fire of Thy Cause.
—*Bahá'u'lláh*

I beseech Thee, O Thou Who art the Lord of all names, to guard Thy loved ones against Thine enemies, and to strengthen them in their love for Thee and in fulfilling Thy pleasure. Do Thou protect them, that their footsteps may slip not, that their hearts may not be shut out as by a veil from Thee, and that their eyes may be restrained from beholding anything that is not of Thee. Cause them to be so enraptured by the sweetness of Thy divine melodies that they will rid themselves of all attachment to any one except Thee, and will turn wholly towards Thee, and extol Thee under all conditions, saying: "Praised be Thou, O Lord our

God, inasmuch as Thou hast enabled us to recognize Thy most exalted and all-glorious Self. We will, by Thy mercy, cleave to Thee, and will detach ourselves from any one but Thee. We have realized that Thou art the Beloved of the worlds and the Creator of earth and heaven!"

Glorified be God, the Lord of all creation!
—Bahá'u'lláh

As to thee, O handmaid of God, softly recite thou this commune to thy Lord, and say unto Him:

O God, my God! Fill up for me the cup of detachment from all things, and in the assembly of Thy splendors and bestowals, rejoice me with the wine of loving Thee. Free me from the assaults of passion and desire, break off from me the shackles of this nether world, draw me with rapture unto Thy supernal realm, and refresh me amongst the handmaids with the breathings of Thy holiness.

O Lord, brighten Thou my face with the lights of Thy bestowals, light Thou mine eyes with beholding the signs of Thine all-subduing might; delight my heart with the glory of Thy knowledge that encompasseth all things, gladden Thou my soul with Thy soul-reviving tidings of great joy, O Thou King of this world and the Kingdom above, O Thou Lord of dominion and might, that I may spread abroad Thy signs and tokens, and proclaim Thy Cause, and promote Thy Teachings, and serve Thy Law, and exalt Thy Word.

Thou art verily the Powerful, the Ever-Giving, the Able, the Omnipotent.

—'Abdu'l-Bahá

ECSTASY!

> . . . sweet is the holy ecstasy if thou drinkest of the mystic chalice from the hands of the celestial Youth. Shouldst thou attain this station, thou wouldst be freed from destruction and death, from toil and sin.
> —Bahá'u'lláh

I beseech Thee, O my Lord, by the name of Him round Whom circleth in adoration the kingdom of Thy names, that Thou wilt graciously assist them that are dear to Thee to glorify Thy word among Thy servants, and to shed abroad Thy praise amidst Thy creatures, so that the ecstasies of Thy revelation may fill the souls of all the dwellers of Thine earth.

—*Bahá'u'lláh*

Praised be Thou, O Lord my God! Every time I am reminded of Thee and muse on Thy virtues, I am seized with such ecstasies and am so enravished by Thee that I find myself unable to make mention of Thy name and to extol Thee. I am carried back to such heights that I recognize my self to be the same as the remembrance of Thee in Thy realm, and the essence of Thy praise among Thy servants. As long as that self endureth, so long will Thy praise continue to be shed abroad among Thy creatures and Thy remembrance glorified by Thy people.
—*Bahá'u'lláh*

Make firm our steps, O Lord, in Thy path and strengthen Thou our hearts in Thine obedience. Turn our faces toward the beauty of Thy oneness, and gladden our bosoms with the signs of Thy divine unity. Adorn our bodies with the robe of Thy bounty, and remove from our eyes the veil of sinfulness, and give us the chalice of Thy grace; that the essence of all beings may sing Thy praise before the vision of Thy grandeur. Reveal then Thyself, O Lord, by Thy merciful utterance and the mystery of Thy divine being, that the holy ecstasy of prayer may fill our souls—a prayer that shall rise above words and letters and transcend the murmur of syllables and sounds—that all things may be merged into nothingness before the revelation of Thy splendor.

Lord! These are servants that have remained fast and firm in Thy Covenant and Thy Testament, that have held fast unto the cord of constancy in Thy Cause and clung unto the hem of the robe of Thy grandeur. Assist them, O Lord, with Thy grace, confirm with Thy power and strengthen their loins in obedience to Thee.

Thou art the Pardoner, the Gracious.

—'Abdu'l-Bahá

By the Ancient Beauty!—may my life be a sacrifice for His loved ones—Were the friends to realize what a glorious sovereignty the Lord hath destined for them in His Kingdom, surely they would be filled with ecstasy, would behold themselves crowned with immortal glory and carried away with transports of delight. Erelong it shall be made manifest how brilliantly the light of His bountiful care and mercy hath shone upon His loved ones, and what a turbulent ocean hath been stirred in their hearts! Then will they clamor and exclaim: Happy are we; let all the world rejoice!

—'Abdu'l-Bahá

Sorrow and Joy

> . . . all the sorrow and the grief that exist come from the world of matter: the spiritual world bestows only the joy!
> —'Abdu'l-Bahá

O God, my God! Be Thou not far from me, for tribulation upon tribulation hath gathered about me. O God, my God! Leave me not to myself, for the extreme of adversity hath come upon me. Out of the pure milk, drawn from the breasts of Thy loving-kindness, give me to drink, for my thirst hath utterly consumed me. Beneath the shadow of the wings of Thy mercy shelter me, for all mine adversaries with one consent have fallen upon me. Keep me near to the throne of Thy majesty, face to face with the revelation of the signs of Thy glory, for wretchedness hath grievously touched me. With the fruits of the Tree of Thine Eternity nourish me, for uttermost weakness hath overtaken me. From the cups of joy, proffered by the hands of Thy tender mercies, feed me, for manifold sorrows have laid mighty hold upon me. With the broidered robe of Thine omnipotent sovereignty attire me, for poverty hath altogether despoiled me. Lulled by the cooing of the Dove of Thine Eternity, suffer me to sleep, for woes at their blackest have befallen me. Before the throne of Thy oneness, amid the blaze of the beauty of Thy countenance, cause me to abide, for fear and trembling have violently crushed me. Beneath the ocean of Thy forgiveness, faced with the restlessness of the leviathan of glory, immerse me, for my sins have utterly doomed me.

—*Bahá'u'lláh*

SORROW AND JOY

O My servants!
Sorrow not if, in these days and on this earthly plane, things contrary to your wishes have been ordained and manifested by God, for days of blissful joy, of heavenly delight, are assuredly in store for you. Worlds, holy and spiritually glorious, will be unveiled to your eyes. You are destined by Him, in this world and hereafter, to partake of their benefits, to share in their joys, and to obtain a portion of their sustaining grace. To each and every one of them you will, no doubt, attain.

—*Bahá'u'lláh*

He is the Compassionate, the All-Bountiful!
O God, my God! Thou seest me, Thou knowest me; Thou art my Haven and my Refuge. None have I sought nor any will I seek save Thee; no path have I trodden nor any will I tread but the path of Thy love. In the darksome night of despair, my eye turneth expec-

tant and full of hope to the morn of Thy boundless favor and at the hour of dawn my drooping soul is refreshed and strengthened in remembrance of Thy beauty and perfection. He whom the grace of Thy mercy aideth, though he be but a drop, shall become the boundless ocean, and the merest atom which the outpouring of Thy loving-kindness assisteth, shall shine even as the radiant star.

    Shelter under Thy protection, O Thou Spirit of purity, Thou Who art the All-Bountiful Provider, this enthralled, enkindled servant of Thine. Aid him in this world of being to remain steadfast and firm in Thy love and grant that this broken-winged bird attain a refuge and shelter in Thy divine nest that abideth upon the celestial tree.

—'Abdu'l-Bahá

O Divine Providence!
   Lift to Thy lovers' lips a cup brimful of

anguish. To the yearners on Thy pathway, make sweetness but a sting, and poison honey-sweet. Set Thou our heads for ornaments on the points of spears. Make Thou our hearts the targets for pitiless arrows and darts. Raise Thou this withered soul to life on the martyr's field, make Thou his faded heart to drink the draught of tyranny, and thus grow fresh and fair once more. Make him to be drunk with the wine of Thine Eternal Covenant, make him a reveller holding high his cup. Help him to fling away his life; grant that for Thy sake, he be offered up.

Thou art the Mighty, the Powerful. Thou art the Knower, the Seer, the Hearer.

—'Abdu'l-Bahá

O Lord, my God and my Haven in my distress! My Shield and my Shelter in my woes! My Asylum and Refuge in time of need and in my loneliness my Companion! In my anguish my Solace, and in my solitude a loving Friend! The Remover of the pangs of my sorrows and the Pardoner of my sins!

Wholly unto Thee do I turn, fervently imploring Thee with all my heart, my mind and my tongue, to shield me from all that runs counter to Thy will in this, the cycle of Thy divine unity, and to cleanse me of all defilement that will hinder me from seeking, stainless and unsullied, the shade of the tree of Thy grace.

Have mercy, O Lord, on the feeble, make whole the sick, and quench the burning thirst.

Gladden the bosom wherein the fire of Thy love doth smolder, and set it aglow with the flame of Thy celestial love and spirit.

Robe the tabernacles of divine unity with the vesture of holiness, and set upon my head the crown of Thy favor.

Illumine my face with the radiance of the orb of Thy bounty, and graciously aid me in ministering at Thy holy threshold.

Make my heart overflow with love for Thy

creatures and grant that I may become the sign of Thy mercy, the token of Thy grace, the promoter of concord amongst Thy loved ones, devoted unto Thee, uttering Thy commemoration and forgetful of self but ever mindful of what is Thine.

O God, my God! Stay not from me the gentle gales of Thy pardon and grace, and deprive me not of the wellsprings of Thine aid and favor.

'Neath the shade of Thy protecting wings let me nestle, and cast upon me the glance of Thine all-protecting eye.

Loose my tongue to laud Thy name amidst Thy people, that my voice may be raised in great assemblies and from my lips may stream the flood of Thy praise.

Thou art, in all truth, the Gracious, the Glorified, the Mighty, the Omnipotent.

—'Abdu'l-Bahá

O sincere servant of the True One! I hear thou art grieved and distressed at the happenings of the world and the vicissitudes of fortune. Wherefore this fear and sorrow? The true lovers of the Abhá Beauty, and they that have quaffed the Cup of the Covenant fear no calamity, nor feel depressed in the hour of trial. They regard the fire of adversity as their garden of delight, and the depth of the sea the expanse of heaven.

Thou who art neath the shelter of God, and under the shadow of the Tree of His Covenant, why sorrow and repine? Rest thou assured and feel confident. Observe the written commandments of thy Lord with joy and peace, with earnestness and sincerity; and be thou the well-wisher of thy country and thy government. His grace shall assist thee at all times, His blessings shall be bestowed upon thee, and thy heart's desire shall be realized.

—'Abdu'l-Bahá

Seeking

Seek whatsoever thou seekest from Him alone.
—'Abdu'l-Bahá

Glorified be Thy name, O Lord my God! I beseech Thee by Thy power that hath encompassed all created things, and by Thy sovereignty that hath transcended the entire creation, and by Thy Word which was hidden in Thy wisdom and whereby Thou didst create Thy heaven and Thy earth, both to enable us to be steadfast in our love for Thee and in our obedience to Thy pleasure, and to fix our gaze upon Thy face, and celebrate Thy glory. Empower us, then, O my God, to spread abroad Thy signs among Thy creatures, and to guard Thy Faith in Thy realm. Thou hast ever existed independently of the mention of any of Thy creatures, and wilt remain as Thou hast been for ever and ever.

In Thee I have placed my whole confidence, unto Thee I have turned my face, to the cord of Thy loving providence I have clung, and towards the shadow of Thy mercy I have hastened. Cast me not as one disappointed out of Thy door, O my God, and withhold not from me Thy grace, for Thee alone do I seek. No God is there beside Thee, the Ever-Forgiving, the Most Bountiful.

Praise be to Thee, O Thou Who art the Beloved of them that have known Thee!
—*Bahá'u'lláh*

O My friend, listen with heart and soul to the songs of the spirit, and treasure them as thine own eyes. For the heavenly wisdoms, like the clouds of spring, will not rain down on the earth of men's hearts forever; and though the grace of the All-Bounteous One is never stilled and never ceasing, yet to each time and era a portion is allotted and a bounty set apart, this in a given measure. "And no one thing is there, but with Us are its storehouses; and We send it not down but in settled measure."* The cloud of the Loved One's mercy raineth only on the garden of the spirit, and bestoweth this bounty only in the season of spring. The other seasons have no share in this greatest grace, and barren lands no portion of this favor.

O Brother! Not every sea hath pearls; not every branch will flower, nor will the nightingale sing thereon. Then, ere the nightingale of the mystic paradise repair to the garden of God, and the rays of the heavenly morning return to the Sun of Truth—make thou an effort, that haply in this dustheap of the mortal world thou mayest catch a fragrance from the everlasting garden, and live forever in the shadow of the peoples of this city. And when thou hast attained this highest station and come to this mightiest plane, then shalt thou gaze on the Beloved, and forget all else.

—*Bahá'u'lláh*

*Qur'an 15:21.

❧

I seek patience only in God. Verily He is the best protector and the best helper. No refuge do I seek save God. Verily He is the guardian and the best supporter. . . .

I swear by the glory of God, My Lord, the Most Exalted, the Most Great, He assuredly, as is divinely ordained, will make His Cause shine resplendent, while there will be no helper for the unjust. . . .

Verily I seek patience only in God, and Him do I regard as the goal of My desire.
—*The Báb*

❧

Verily I am Thy servant, O my God, and Thy poor one and Thy suppliant and Thy wretched creature. I have arrived at Thy gate, seeking Thy shelter.

I have found no contentment save in Thy love, no exultation except in Thy remembrance, no eagerness but in obedience to Thee, no joy save in Thy nearness, and no tranquillity except in reunion with Thee, notwithstanding that I am conscious that all created things are debarred from Thy sublime Essence and the entire creation is denied access to Thine inmost Being. Whenever I attempt to approach Thee, I perceive nothing in myself but the tokens of Thy grace and behold naught in my being but the revelations of Thy lovingkindness.

How can one who is but Thy creature seek reunion with Thee and attain unto Thy presence, whereas no created thing can ever be associated with Thee, nor can aught comprehend Thee? How is it possible for a lowly servant to recognize Thee and to extol Thy praise, notwithstanding that Thou hast destined for him the revelations of Thy dominion and the wondrous testimonies of Thy sovereignty? Thus every created thing beareth witness that it is debarred from the sanctuary of Thy presence by reason of the limitations imposed upon its inner reality.

It is undisputed, however, that the influence of Thine attraction hath everlastingly been inherent in the realities of Thy handiwork, although that which beseemeth the hallowed court of Thy providence is exalted beyond the attainment of the entire creation. This indicateth, O my God, my utter powerlessness to praise Thee and revealeth my utmost impotence in yielding thanks unto Thee; and how much more to attain the recognition of Thy divine unity or to succeed in reaching the clear tokens of Thy praise, Thy sanctity and Thy glory.

Nay, by Thy might, I yearn for naught but Thine Own Self and seek no one other than Thee.

— *The Báb*

O holy Lord! O Lord of loving-kindness! We stray about Thy dwelling, longing to behold Thy beauty, and loving all Thy ways.

We are hapless, lowly, and of small account. We are paupers: show us mercy, give us bounty; look not upon our failings, hide Thou our endless sins. Whatever we are, still are we Thine, and what we speak and hear is praise of Thee, and it is Thy face we seek, Thy path we follow. Thou art the Lord of loving-kindness, we are sinners and astray and far from home.

Wherefore, O Cloud of Mercy, grant us some drops of rain. O Flowering Bed of grace, send forth a fragrant breeze. O Sea of all bestowals, roll towards us a great wave. O Sun of Bounty, send down a shaft of light. Grant us pity, grant us grace.

—'Abdu'l-Bahá

Gathering

Do not call it a meeting. Call it a confluence of holy souls; a convocation of those who love the Lord; a retreat for the people of the All-Merciful; a palace-hall for all who sing His praise.
—'Abdu'l-Bahá

Through the movement of Our Pen of glory We have, at the bidding of the omnipotent Ordainer, breathed a new life into every human frame, and instilled into every word a fresh potency. All created things proclaim the evidences of this world-wide regeneration. This is the most great, the most joyful tidings imparted by the Pen of this Wronged One to mankind.

Wherefore fear ye, O My well-beloved ones?

Who is it that can dismay you? A touch of moisture sufficeth to dissolve the hardened clay out of which this perverse generation is molded. The mere act of your gathering together is enough to scatter the forces of these vain and worthless people.

— *Bahá'u'lláh*

❦

O God, my God! These are Thy feeble servants; they are Thy loyal bondsmen and Thy handmaidens, who have bowed themselves down before Thine exalted Utterance and humbled themselves at Thy Threshold of light, and borne witness to Thy oneness through which the Sun hath been made to shine in midday splendor. They have listened to the summons Thou didst raise from out Thy hidden Realm, and with hearts quivering with love and rapture, they have responded to Thy call.

O Lord, shower upon them all the outpourings of Thy mercy, rain down upon them all the waters of Thy grace. Make them to grow as beauteous plants in the garden of heaven, and from the full and brimming clouds of Thy bestowals and out of the deep pools of Thine abounding grace make Thou this garden to flower and keep it ever green and lustrous, ever fresh and shimmering and fair.

Thou art verily the Mighty, the Exalted, the Powerful, He Who alone, in the heavens and on the earth, abideth unchanged. There is none other God save Thee, the Lord of manifest tokens and signs.

— 'Abdu'l‑Bahá

O Thou Lord of the Kingdom! Though our bodies be gathered here together, yet our spellbound hearts are carried away by Thy love, and yet are we transported by the rays of Thy resplendent face. Weak though we be, we await the revelations of Thy might and power. Poor though we be, with neither goods nor means, still take we riches from the treasures of Thy Kingdom. Drops though we be, still do we draw from out Thy ocean deeps. Motes though we be, still do we gleam in the glory of Thy splendid Sun.

O Thou our Provider! Send down Thine aid, that each one gathered here may become a lighted candle, each one a center of attraction, each one a summoner to Thy heavenly realms, till at last we make this nether world the mirror image of Thy Paradise.
— 'Abdu'l-Bahá

When you present yourselves in the meetings, before entering them, free yourselves from all that you have in your heart, free your thoughts and your minds from all else save God, and speak to your heart. That all may make this a gathering of love, make it the cause of illumination, make it a gathering of attraction of the hearts, surround this gathering with the Lights of the Supreme Concourse, so that you may be gathered together with the utmost love:

O God! Dispel all those elements which are the cause of discord, and prepare for us all those things which are the cause of unity and accord!

O God! Descend upon us Heavenly Fragrance and change this gathering into a gathering of Heaven! Grant to us every benefit and every food. Prepare for us the Food of Love! Give to us the Food of Knowledge! Bestow upon us the Food of Heavenly Illumination!

In your hearts remember these things, and then enter the Unity Feast.

— 'Abdu'l-Bahá

Meditations

*Put away the cups of Paradise
and all the life-giving waters they contain,
for lo,
the people of Bahá
have entered the blissful abode
of the Divine Presence,
and quaffed the wine of reunion
from the chalice
of the beauty of their Lord,
the All-Possessing, the Most High.*
—Bahá'u'lláh

ALLÁH-U ABHÁ!

Alláh-u Abhá* is an Arabic phrase meaning "God the All-Glorious." In Islam, there is a tradition that among the many names of God, one is the Greatest Name; but the identity of this Greatest Name is hidden. Bahá'u'lláh has stated that the Greatest Name of God is "Bahá" (Glory, Light, Splendor). "Abhá" (Most Glorious, All-Glorious) is a form of the Greatest Name.

It hath been ordained that every believer in God, the Lord of Judgment, shall, each day, having washed his hands and then his face, seat himself and, turning unto God,† repeat:

Alláh-u Abhá

---

*Pronounced: al-AHH-ho ab-HA.
†That is, turning toward the Qiblih, the Point of Adoration; today, the Shrine of Bahá'u'lláh.

ninety-five times. Such was the decree of the Maker of the Heavens when, with majesty and power, He established Himself upon the thrones of His Names.

—Bahá'u'lláh

Tablet of Aḥmad

. . .the Tablet of Aḥmad [has] been invested by Bahá'u'lláh with a special potency and significance, and should therefore be accepted as such and be recited by the believers with unquestioning faith and confidence, that through them they may enter into a much closer communion with God, and identify themselves more fully with His laws and precepts.
—from a letter written on behalf of Shoghi Effendi

He is the King, the All-Knowing, the Wise! Lo, the Nightingale of Paradise singeth upon the twigs of the Tree of Eternity, with holy and sweet melodies, proclaiming to the sincere ones the glad tidings of the nearness of God, calling the believers in the Divine Unity to the court of the Presence of the Generous

One, informing the severed ones of the message which hath been revealed by God, the King, the Glorious, the Peerless, guiding the lovers to the seat of sanctity and to this resplendent Beauty.

Verily this is that Most Great Beauty, foretold in the Books of the Messengers, through Whom truth shall be distinguished from error and the wisdom of every command shall be tested. Verily He is the Tree of Life that bringeth forth the fruits of God, the Exalted, the Powerful, the Great.

O Aḥmad! Bear thou witness that verily He is God and there is no God but Him, the King, the Protector, the Incomparable, the Omnipotent. And that the One Whom He hath sent forth by the name of 'Alí* was the true One from God, to Whose commands we are all conforming.

Say: O people be obedient to the ordinances of God, which have been enjoined in

---

*The Báb

the Bayan by the Glorious, the Wise One. Verily He is the King of the Messengers and His Book is the Mother Book did ye but know.

Thus doth the Nightingale utter His call unto you from this prison. He hath but to deliver this clear message. Whosoever desireth, let him turn aside from this counsel and whosoever desireth let him choose the path to his Lord.

O people, if ye deny these verses, by what proof have ye believed in God? Produce it, O assemblage of false ones.

Nay, by the One in Whose hand is my soul, they are not, and never shall be able to do this, even should they combine to assist one another.

O Aḥmad! Forget not My bounties while I am absent. Remember My days during thy days, and My distress and banishment in this remote prison. And be thou so steadfast in My love that thy heart shall not waver, even if the swords of the enemies rain blows upon thee and all the heavens and the earth arise against thee.

Be thou as a flame of fire to My enemies and a river of life eternal to My loved ones, and be not of those who doubt.

And if thou art overtaken by affliction in My path, or degradation for My sake, be not thou troubled thereby.

Rely upon God, thy God and the Lord of thy fathers. For the people are wandering in the paths of delusion, bereft of discernment to see God with their own eyes, or hear His Melody with their own ears. Thus have We found them, as thou also dost witness.

Thus have their superstitions become veils between them and their own hearts and kept them from the path of God, the Exalted, the Great.

Be thou assured in thyself that verily, he who turns away from this Beauty hath also turned away from the Messengers of the past and showeth pride towards God from all eternity to all eternity.

Learn well this Tablet, O Aḥmad. Chant it during thy days and withhold not thyself therefrom. For verily, God hath ordained for the one who chants it, the reward of a hundred martyrs and a service in both worlds. These favors have We bestowed upon thee as a bounty on Our part and a mercy from Our presence, that thou mayest be of those who are grateful.

By God! Should one who is in affliction or grief read this Tablet with absolute sincerity, God will dispel his sadness, solve his difficulties and remove his afflictions.

Verily, He is the Merciful, the Compassionate. Praise be to God, the Lord of all the worlds.

—Bahá'u'lláh

Long Healing Prayer

. . .the Healing Prayer [has] been invested by Bahá'u'lláh with a special potency and significance, and should therefore be accepted as such and be recited by the believers with unquestioning faith and confidence, that through them they may enter into a much closer communion with God, and identify themselves more fully with His laws and precepts.
—from a letter written on behalf of Shoghi Effendi

He is the Healer, the Sufficer, the Helper, the All-Forgiving, the All-Merciful.

I call on Thee O Exalted One, O Faithful One, O Glorious One! Thou the Sufficing, Thou the Healing, Thou the Abiding, O Thou Abiding One!

I call on Thee O Sovereign, O Upraiser, O Judge! Thou the Sufficing, Thou the Healing, Thou the Abiding, O Thou Abiding One!

I call on Thee O Peerless One, O Eternal One, O Single One! Thou the Sufficing, Thou the Healing, Thou the Abiding, O Thou Abiding One!

I call on Thee O Most Praised One, O Holy One, O Helping One! Thou the Sufficing, Thou the Healing, Thou the Abiding, O Thou Abiding One!

I call on Thee O Omniscient, O Most Wise, O Most Great One! Thou the Sufficing, Thou the Healing, Thou the Abiding, O Thou Abiding One!

I call on Thee O Clement One, O Majestic One, O Ordaining One! Thou the Sufficing, Thou the Healing, Thou the Abiding, O Thou Abiding One!

I call on Thee O Beloved One, O Cherished One, O Enraptured One! Thou the Sufficing, Thou the Healing, Thou the Abiding, O Thou Abiding One!

I call on Thee O Mightiest One, O Sustaining One, O Potent One! Thou the Sufficing, Thou the Healing, Thou the Abiding, O Thou Abiding One!

I call on Thee O Ruling One, O Self-Subsisting, O All-Knowing One! Thou the Sufficing, Thou the Healing, Thou the Abiding, O Thou Abiding One!

I call on Thee O Spirit, O Light, O Most Manifest One! Thou the Sufficing, Thou the Healing, Thou the Abiding, O Thou Abiding One!

I call on Thee O Thou Frequented by all, O Thou Known to all, O Thou Hidden from all! Thou the Sufficing, Thou the Healing, Thou the Abiding, O Thou Abiding One!

I call on Thee O Concealed One, O Triumphant One, O Bestowing One! Thou the Sufficing, Thou the Healing, Thou the Abiding, O Thou Abiding One!

I call on Thee O Almighty, O Succoring One, O Concealing One! Thou the Sufficing, Thou the Healing, Thou the Abiding, O Thou Abiding One!

I call on Thee O Fashioner, O Satisfier, O Uprooter! Thou the Sufficing, Thou the Healing, Thou the Abiding, O Thou Abiding One!

I call on Thee O Rising One, O Gathering One, O Exalting One! Thou the Sufficing, Thou the Healing, Thou the Abiding, O Thou Abiding One!

I call on Thee O Perfecting One, O Unfettered One, O Bountiful One! Thou the Sufficing, Thou the Healing, Thou the Abiding, O Thou Abiding One!

I call on Thee O Beneficent One, O Withholding One, O Creating One! Thou the Sufficing, Thou the Healing, Thou the Abiding, O Thou Abiding One!

I call on Thee O Most Sublime One, O Beauteous One, O Bounteous One! Thou the Sufficing, Thou the Healing, Thou the Abiding, O Thou Abiding One!

I call on Thee O Just One, O Gracious One, O Generous One! Thou the Sufficing, Thou the Healing, Thou the Abiding, O Thou Abiding One!

I call on Thee O All-Compelling, O Ever-Abiding, O Most Knowing One! Thou the Sufficing, Thou the Healing, Thou the Abiding, O Thou Abiding One!

I call on Thee O Magnificent One, O Ancient of Days, O Magnanimous One! Thou the Sufficing, Thou the Healing, Thou the Abiding, O Thou Abiding One!

I call on Thee O Well-guarded One, O Lord of Joy, O Desired One! Thou the Sufficing, Thou the Healing, Thou the Abiding, O Thou Abiding One!

I call on Thee O Thou Kind to all, O Thou Compassionate with all, O Most Benevolent One! Thou the Sufficing, Thou the Healing, Thou the Abiding, O Thou Abiding One!

I call on Thee O Haven for all, O Shelter to all, O All-Preservng One! Thou the Sufficing, Thou the Healing, Thou the Abiding, O Thou Abiding One!

I call on Thee, O Thou Succorer of all, O Thou Invoked by all, O Quickening One! Thou the Sufficing, Thou the Healing, Thou the Abiding, O Thou Abiding One!

I call on Thee O Unfolder, O Ravager, O

Most Clement One! Thou the Sufficing, Thou the Healing, Thou the Abiding, O Thou Abiding One!

I call on Thee O Thou my Soul, O Thou my Beloved, O Thou my Faith! Thou the Sufficing, Thou the Healing, Thou the Abiding, O Thou Abiding One!

I call on Thee O Quencher of thirsts, O Transcendent Lord, O Most Precious One! Thou the Sufficing, Thou the Healing, Thou the Abiding, O Thou Abiding One!

I call on Thee O Greatest Remembrance, O Noblest Name, O Most Ancient Way! Thou the Sufficing, Thou the Healing, Thou the Abiding, O Thou Abiding One!

I call on Thee O Most Lauded, O Most Holy, O Sanctified One! Thou the Sufficing, Thou the Healing, Thou the Abiding, O Thou Abiding One!

I call on Thee O Unfastener, O Counselor, O Deliverer! Thou the Sufficing, Thou the Healing, Thou the Abiding, O Thou Abiding One!

I call on Thee O Friend, O Physician, O Captivating One! Thou the Sufficing, Thou the Healing, Thou the Abiding, O Thou Abiding One!

I call on Thee O Glory, O Beauty, O Bountiful One! Thou the Sufficing, Thou the Healing, Thou the Abiding, O Thou Abiding One!

I call on Thee O the Most Trusted, O the Best Lover, O Lord of the Dawn! Thou the Sufficing, Thou the Healing, Thou the Abiding, O Thou Abiding One!

I call on Thee O Enkindler, O Brightener, O Bringer of Delight! Thou the Sufficing, Thou the Healing, Thou the Abiding, O Thou Abiding One!

I call on Thee O Lord of Bounty, O Most Compassionate, O Most Merciful One! Thou the Sufficing, Thou the Healing, Thou the Abiding, O Thou Abiding One!

I call on Thee O Constant One, O Life-giving One, O Source of all Being! Thou the Sufficing, Thou the Healing, Thou the Abiding, O Thou Abiding One!

I call on Thee O Thou Who penetratest all things, O All-Seeing God, O Lord of Utterance! Thou the Sufficing, Thou the Healing, Thou the Abiding, O Thou Abiding One!

I call on Thee O Manifest yet Hidden, O Unseen yet Renowned, O Onlooker sought by all! Thou the Sufficing, Thou the Healing, Thou the Abiding, O Thou Abiding One!

I call on Thee O Thou Who slayest the Lovers, O God of Grace to the wicked!

O Sufficer, I call on Thee, O Sufficer!
O Healer, I call on Thee, O Healer!
O Abider, I call on Thee, O Abider!
Thou the Ever-Abiding, O Thou Abiding One!

Sanctified art Thou, O my God! I beseech Thee by Thy generosity, whereby the portals of Thy bounty and grace were opened wide, whereby the Temple of Thy Holiness was established upon the throne of eternity; and by Thy mercy whereby Thou didst invite all created things unto the table of Thy bounties and bestowals; and by Thy grace whereby Thou didst respond, in Thine own Self with Thy word "Yea!" on behalf of all in heaven and earth, at the hour when Thy sovereignty and

Thy grandeur stood revealed, at the dawn-time when the might of Thy dominion was made manifest. And again do I beseech Thee, by these most beauteous names, by these most noble and sublime attributes, and by Thy most Exalted Remembrance, and by Thy pure and spotless Beauty, and by Thy hidden Light in the most hidden pavilion, and by Thy Name, cloaked with the garment of affliction every morn and eve, to protect the bearer of this blessed Tablet, and whoso reciteth it, and whoso cometh upon it, and whoso passeth around the house wherein it is. Heal Thou, then, by it every sick, diseased and poor one, from every tribulation and distress, from every loathsome affliction and sorrow, and guide Thou by it whosoever desireth to enter upon the paths of Thy guidance, and the ways of Thy forgiveness and grace.

 Thou art verily the Powerful, the All-Sufficing, the Healing, the Protector, the Giving, the Compassionate, the All-Generous, the All-Merciful.

—*Bahá'u'lláh*

Fire Tablet

Should all the servants read and ponder this, there shall be kindled in their veins a fire that shall set aflame the worlds.
—Bahá'u'lláh

In the Name of God, the Most Ancient, the Most Great.

Indeed the hearts of the sincere are consumed in the fire of separation: Where is the gleaming of the light of Thy Countenance, O Beloved of the worlds?

Those who are near unto Thee have been abandoned in the darkness of desolation: Where is the shining of the morn of Thy reunion, O Desire of the worlds?

The bodies of Thy chosen ones lie quivering on distant sands: Where is the ocean of Thy presence, O Enchanter of the worlds?

Longing hands are uplifted to the heaven of Thy grace and generosity: Where are the rains of Thy bestowal, O Answerer of the worlds?

The infidels have arisen in tyranny on every hand: Where is the compelling power of Thine ordaining pen, O Conqueror of the worlds?

The barking of dogs is loud on every side: Where is the lion of the forest of Thy might, O Chastiser of the worlds?

Coldness hath gripped all mankind: Where is the warmth of Thy love, O Fire of the worlds?

Calamity hath reached its height: Where are the signs of Thy succor, O Salvation of the worlds?

Darkness hath enveloped most of the peoples: Where is the brightness of Thy splendor, O Radiance of the worlds?

The necks of men are stretched out in malice: Where are the swords of Thy vengeance, O Destroyer of the worlds?

Abasement hath reached its lowest depth: Where are the emblems of Thy glory, O Glory of the worlds?

Sorrows have afflicted the Revealer of Thy Name, the All-Merciful: Where is the joy of the Dayspring of Thy Revelation, O Delight of the worlds?

Anguish hath befallen all the peoples of the earth: Where are the ensigns of Thy gladness, O Joy of the worlds?

Thou seest the Dawning Place of Thy signs veiled by evil suggestions: Where are the fingers of Thy might, O Power of the worlds?

Sore thirst hath overcome all men: Where is the river of Thy bounty, O Mercy of the worlds?

Greed hath made captive all mankind: Where are the embodiments of detachment, O Lord of the worlds?

Thou seest this Wronged One lonely in exile: Where are the hosts of the heaven of Thy Command, O Sovereign of the worlds?

I have been forsaken in a foreign land:

Where are the emblems of Thy faithfulness, O Trust of the worlds?

The agonies of death have laid hold on all men: Where is the surging of Thine ocean of eternal life, O Life of the worlds?

The whisperings of Satan have been breathed to every creature: Where is the meteor of Thy fire, O Light of the worlds?

The drunkenness of passion hath perverted most of mankind: Where are the daysprings of purity, O Desire of the worlds?

Thou seest this Wronged One veiled in tyranny among the Syrians: Where is the radiance of Thy dawning light, O Light of the worlds?

Thou seest Me forbidden to speak forth: Then from where will spring Thy melodies, O Nightingale of the worlds?

Most of the people are enwrapped in fancy and idle imaginings: Where are the exponents of Thy certitude, O Assurance of the worlds?

Bahá is drowning in a sea of tribulation: Where is the Ark of Thy salvation, O Savior of the worlds?

Thou seest the Dayspring of Thine utterance in the darkness of creation: Where is the sun of the heaven of Thy grace, O Lightgiver of the worlds?

The lamps of truth and purity, of loyalty and honor, have been put out: Where are the signs of Thine avenging wrath, O Mover of the worlds?

Canst Thou see any who have championed Thy Self, or who ponder on what hath befallen Him in the pathway of Thy love? Now doth My pen halt, O Beloved of the worlds.

The branches of the Divine Lote-Tree lie broken by the onrushing gales of destiny: Where are the banners of Thy succor, O Champion of the worlds?

This Face is hidden in the dust of slander: Where are the breezes of Thy compassion, O Mercy of the worlds?

The robe of sanctity is sullied by the people of deceit: Where is the vesture of Thy holiness, O Adorner of the worlds?

The sea of grace is stilled for what the

hands of men have wrought: Where are the waves of Thy bounty, O Desire of the worlds?

The door leading to the Divine Presence is locked through the tyranny of Thy foes: Where is the key of Thy bestowal, O Unlocker of the worlds?

The leaves are yellowed by the poisoning winds of sedition: Where is the downpour of the clouds of Thy bounty, O Giver of the worlds?

The universe is darkened with the dust of sin: Where are the breezes of Thy forgiveness, O Forgiver of the worlds?

This Youth is lonely in a desolate land: Where is the rain of Thy heavenly grace, O Bestower of the worlds?

O Supreme Pen, We have heard Thy most sweet call in the eternal realm: Give Thou ear unto what the Tongue of Grandeur uttereth, O Wronged One of the worlds!

Were it not for the cold, how would the heat of Thy words prevail, O Expounder of the worlds?

Were it not for calamity, how would the sun of Thy patience shine, O Light of the worlds? Lament not because of the wicked. Thou wert created to bear and endure, O Patience of the worlds.

How sweet was Thy dawning on the horizon of the Covenant among the stirrers of sedition, and Thy yearning after God, O Love of the worlds.

By Thee the banner of independence was planted on the highest peaks, and the sea of bounty surged, O Rapture of the worlds.

By Thine aloneness the Sun of Oneness shone, and by Thy banishment the land of Unity was adorned. Be patient, O Thou Exile of the worlds.

We have made abasement the garment of glory, and affliction the adornment of Thy temple, O Pride of the worlds.

Thou seest the hearts are filled with hate, and to overlook is Thine, O Thou Concealer of the sins of the worlds.

When the swords flash, go forward! When

the shafts fly, press onward! O Thou Sacrifice of the worlds.

Dost Thou wail, or shall I wail? Rather shall I weep at the fewness of Thy champions,

O Thou Who hast caused the wailing of the worlds.

Verily, I have heard Thy Call, O All-Glorious Beloved; and now is the face of Bahá flaming with the heat of tribulation and with the fire of Thy shining word, and He hath risen up in faithfulness at the place of sacrifice, looking toward Thy pleasure, O Ordainer of the worlds.

O 'Alí-Akbar, thank thy Lord for this Tablet whence thou canst breathe the fragrance of My meekness, and know what hath beset Us in the path of God, the Adored of all the worlds.

Should all the servants read and ponder this, there shall be kindled in their veins a fire that shall set aflame the worlds.

— *Bahá'u'lláh*

Tablet of the Holy Mariner

Study the Tablet of the Holy Mariner that ye may know the truth, and consider that the Blessed Beauty hath fully foretold future events. Let them who perceive, take warning!
— 'Abdu'l-Bahá

He is the Gracious, the Well-Beloved!

O Holy Mariner! Bid thine ark of eternity appear before the Celestial Concourse.

Glorified be my Lord, the All-Glorious!

Launch it upon the ancient sea, in His Name, the Most Wondrous,

Glorified be my Lord, the All-Glorious!

And let the angelic spirits enter, in the Name of God, the Most High.

Glorified be my Lord, the All-Glorious!

Unmoor it, then, that it may sail upon the ocean of glory,
    Glorified be my Lord, the All-Glorious!
Haply the dwellers therein may attain the retreats of nearness in the everlasting realm.
    Glorified be my Lord, the All-Glorious!
Having reached the sacred strand, the shore of the crimson seas,
    Glorified be my Lord, the All-Glorious!
Bid them issue forth and attain this ethereal invisible station,
    Glorified be my Lord, the All-Glorious!
A station wherein the Lord hath in the Flame of His Beauty appeared within the deathless tree;
    Glorified be my Lord, the All-Glorious!
Wherein the embodiments of His Cause cleansed themselves of self and passion;
    Glorified be my Lord, the All-Glorious!
Around which the Glory of Moses doth circle with the everlasting hosts;
    Glorified be my Lord, the All-Glorious!
Wherein the Hand of God was drawn forth from His bosom of Grandeur;

Glorified be my Lord, the All-Glorious! Wherein the ark of the Cause remaineth motionless even though to its dwellers be declared all divine attributes.

Glorified be my Lord, the All-Glorious! O Mariner! Teach them that are within the ark that which we have taught thee behind the mystic veil,

Glorified be my Lord, the All-Glorious! Perchance they may not tarry in the sacred snow-white spot,

Glorified be my Lord, the All-Glorious! But may soar upon the wings of the spirit unto that station which the Lord hath exalted above all mention in the worlds below,

Glorified be my Lord, the All-Glorious! May wing through space even as the favored birds in the realm of eternal reunion;

Glorified be my Lord, the All-Glorious! May know the mysteries hidden in the Seas of light.

Glorified be my Lord, the All-Glorious! They passed the grades of worldly limitations and reached that of the divine unity, the center of heavenly guidance.

Glorified be my Lord, the All-Glorious!
They have desired to ascend unto that state which the Lord hath ordained to be above their stations.

Glorified be my Lord, the All-Glorious!
Whereupon the burning meteor cast them out from them that abide in the Kingdom of His Presence,

Glorified be my Lord, the All-Glorious!
And they heard the Voice of Grandeur raised from behind the unseen pavilion upon the Height of Glory:

Glorified be my Lord, the All-Glorious!
"O guardian angels! Return them to their abode in the world below,

Glorified be my Lord, the All-Glorious!
"Inasmuch as they have purposed to rise to that sphere which the wings of the celestial dove have never attained;

Glorified be my Lord, the All-Glorious!
"Whereupon the ship of fancy standeth still

which the minds of them that comprehend cannot grasp."

Glorified be my Lord, the All-Glorious! Whereupon the maid of heaven looked out from her exalted chamber,

Glorified be my Lord, the All-Glorious! And with her brow signed to the Celestial Concourse,

Glorified be my Lord, the All-Glorious! Flooding with the light of her countenance the heaven and the earth,

Glorified be my Lord, the All-Glorious! And as the radiance of her beauty shone upon the people of dust,

Glorified be my Lord, the All-Glorious! All beings were shaken in their mortal graves.

Glorified be my Lord, the All-Glorious! She then raised the call which no ear through all eternity hath ever heard,

Glorified be my Lord, the All-Glorious! And thus proclaimed: "By the Lord! He whose heart hath not the fragrance of the love of the exalted and glorious Arabian Youth,

Glorified be my Lord, the All-Glorious! "Can in no wise ascend unto the glory of the highest heaven."

Glorified be my Lord, the All-Glorious! Thereupon she summoned unto herself one maiden from her handmaidens,

Glorified be my Lord, the All-Glorious! And commanded her: "Descend into space from the mansions of eternity,

Glorified be my Lord, the All-Glorious! "And turn thou unto that which they have concealed in the inmost of their hearts.

Glorified be my Lord, the All-Glorious! "Shouldst thou inhale the perfume of the robe from the Youth that hath been hidden within the tabernacle of light by reason of that which the hands of the wicked have wrought,

Glorified be my Lord, the All-Glorious! "Raise a cry within thyself, that all the inmates of the chambers of Paradise, that are the embodiments of the eternal wealth, may understand and hearken;

Glorified be my Lord, the All-Glorious!

"That they may all come down from their everlasting chambers and tremble,
   Glorified be my Lord, the All-Glorious!
"And kiss their hands and feet for having soared to the heights of faithfulness;
   Glorified be my Lord, the All-Glorious!
"Perchance they may find from their robes the fragrance of the Beloved One."
   Glorified be my Lord, the All-Glorious!
Thereupon the countenance of the favored damsel beamed above the celestial chambers even as the light that shineth from the face of the Youth above His mortal temple;
   Glorified be my Lord, the All-Glorious!
She then descended with such an adorning as to illumine the heavens and all that is therein.
   Glorified be my Lord, the All-Glorious!
She bestirred herself and perfumed all things in the lands of holiness and grandeur.
   Glorified be my Lord, the All-Glorious!
When she reached that place she rose to her full height in the midmost heart of creation,
   Glorified be my Lord, the All-Glorious!

And sought to inhale their fragrance at a time that knoweth neither beginning nor end.

 Glorified be my Lord, the All-Glorious!

She found not in them that which she did desire, and this, verily, is but one of His wondrous tales.

 Glorified be my Lord, the All-Glorious!

She then cried aloud, wailed and repaired to her own station within her most lofty mansion,

 Glorified be my Lord, the All-Glorious!

And then gave utterance to one mystic word, whispered privily by her honeyed tongue,

 Glorified be my Lord, the All-Glorious!

And raised the call amidst the Celestial Concourse and the immortal maids of heaven:

 Glorified be my Lord, the All-Glorious!

"By the Lord! I found not from these idle claimants the breeze of Faithfulness!

 Glorified be my Lord, the All-Glorious!

"By the Lord! The Youth hath remained lone and forlorn in the land of exile in the hands of the ungodly."

 Glorified be my Lord, the All-Glorious!

She then uttered within herself such a cry that the Celestial Concourse did shriek and tremble,
    Glorified be my Lord, the All-Glorious!
And she fell upon the dust and gave up the spirit. It seemeth she was called and hearkened unto Him that summoned her unto the Realm on High.
    Glorified be my Lord, the All-Glorious!
Glorified be He that created her out of the essence of love in the midmost heart of his exalted paradise!
    Glorified be my Lord, the All-Glorious!
Thereupon the maids of heaven hastened forth from their chambers, upon whose countenances the eye of no dweller in the highest paradise had ever gazed.
    Glorified be our Lord, the Most High!
They all gathered around her, and lo! they found her body fallen upon the dust;
    Glorified be our Lord, the Most High!
And as they beheld her state and comprehended a word of the tale told by the Youth, they

bared their heads, rent their garments asunder, beat upon their faces, forgot their joy, shed tears and smote with their hands upon their cheeks, and this is verily one of the mysterious grievous afflictions—

Glorified be our Lord, the Most High!
—*Bahá'u'lláh*

Tablet of the True Seeker

The following passage, which has become known as the Tablet of the True Seeker in the West, is an excerpt from the Kitáb-i Íqán.

O my brother, when a true seeker determineth to take the step of search in the path leading to the knowledge of the Ancient of Days, he must, before all else, cleanse and purify his heart, which is the seat of the revelation of the inner mysteries of God, from the obscuring dust of all acquired knowledge, and the allusions of the embodiments of satanic fancy. He must purge his breast, which is the sanctuary of the abiding love of the Beloved, of every defilement, and sanctify his soul from all that pertaineth to water and clay, from all shadowy and ephemeral attachments. He must so cleanse his heart that no remnant of either love or hate may linger therein, lest that love blindly incline him to error, or that hate repel him away from the truth. Even as thou dost witness in this day how most of the people, because of such love and hate, are bereft of the immortal Face, have strayed far from the Embodiments of the divine mysteries, and, shepherdless, are roaming through the wilderness of oblivion and error. That seeker must at all times put his trust in God, must renounce the peoples of the earth, detach himself from the world of dust, and cleave unto Him Who is the Lord of Lords. He must never seek to exalt himself above any one, must wash away from the tablet of his heart every trace of pride and vainglory, must cling unto patience and resignation, observe silence, and refrain from idle talk. For the tongue is a smoldering fire, and excess of speech a deadly poison. Material fire consumeth the body, whereas the fire of the tongue devoureth both heart and soul. The force of the former lasteth but for a time, whilst the effects of the latter endure a century.

That seeker should also regard backbiting as grievous error, and keep himself aloof from its dominion, inasmuch as backbiting quencheth the light of the heart, and extinguisheth the life of the soul. He should be content with little, and be freed from all inordinate desire. He should treasure the companionship of those that have renounced the world, and regard avoidance of boastful and worldly people a precious benefit. At the dawn of every day he should commune with God, and with all his soul persevere in the quest of his Beloved. He should consume every wayward thought with the flame of His loving mention, and, with the swiftness of lightning, pass by all else save Him. He should succor the dispossessed, and never withhold his favor from the destitute. He should show kindness to animals, how much more unto his fellow-man, to him who is endowed with the power of utterance. He should not hesitate to offer up his life for his Beloved, nor allow the censure of the people to turn him away from the Truth. He should not wish for others that which he doth not wish for himself, nor promise that which he doth not fulfil. With all his heart should the seeker avoid fellowship with evil doers, and pray for the remission of their sins. He should forgive the sinful, and never despise his low estate, for none knoweth what his own end shall be. How often hath a sinner, at the hour of death, attained to the essence of faith, and, quaffing the immortal draught, hath taken his flight unto the celestial Concourse. And how often hath a devout believer, at the hour of his soul's ascension, been so changed as to fall into the nethermost fire. Our purpose in revealing these convincing and weighty utterances is to impress upon the seeker that he should regard all else beside God as transient, and count all things save Him, Who is the Object of all adoration, as utter nothingness.

These are among the attributes of the

exalted, and constitute the hall-mark of the spiritually-minded. They have already been mentioned in connection with the requirements of the wayfarers that tread the Path of Positive Knowledge. When the detached wayfarer and sincere seeker hath fulfilled these essential conditions, then and only then can he be called a true seeker. Whensoever he hath fulfilled the conditions implied in the verse: "Whoso maketh efforts for Us," he shall enjoy the blessing conferred by the words: "In Our ways shall We assuredly guide him."

Only when the lamp of search, of earnest striving, of longing desire, of passionate devotion, of fervid love, of rapture, and ecstasy, is kindled within the seeker's heart, and the breeze of His loving-kindness is wafted upon his soul, will the darkness of error be dispelled, the mists of doubts and misgivings be dissipated, and the lights of knowledge and certitude envelop his being. At that hour will the mystic Herald, bearing the joyful tidings of the Spirit, shine forth from the City of God resplendent as the morn, and, through the trumpet-blast of knowledge, will awaken the heart, the soul, and the spirit from the slumber of negligence. Then will the manifold favors and outpouring grace of the holy and everlasting Spirit confer such new life upon the seeker that he will find himself endowed with a new eye, a new ear, a new heart, and a new mind. He will contemplate the manifest signs of the universe, and will penetrate the hidden mysteries of the soul. Gazing with the eye of God, he will perceive within every atom a door that leadeth him to the stations of absolute certitude. He will discover in all things the mysteries of divine Revelation and the evidences of an everlasting manifestation.

I swear by God! Were he that treadeth the path of guidance and seeketh to scale the heights of righteousness to attain unto this glorious and supreme station, he would inhale at a distance of a thousand leagues the fragrance of God, and would perceive the resplendent morn of a divine Guidance rising above the dayspring of all things. Each and every thing, however small, would be to him a revelation, leading him to his Beloved, the Object of his quest. So great shall be the discernment of this seeker that he will discriminate between truth and falsehood even as he doth distinguish the sun from shadow. If in the uttermost corners of the East the sweet savors of God be wafted, he will assuredly recognize and inhale their fragrance, even though he be dwelling in the uttermost ends of the West. He will likewise clearly distinguish all the signs of God—His wondrous utterances, His great works, and mighty deeds—from the doings, words and ways of men, even as the jeweler who knoweth the gem from the stone, or the man who distinguisheth the spring from autumn and heat from cold. When the channel of the human soul is cleansed of all worldly and impeding attachments, it will unfailingly perceive the breath of the Beloved across immeasurable distances, and will, led by its perfume, attain and enter the City of Certitude. Therein he will discern the wonders of His ancient wisdom, and will perceive all the hidden teachings from the rustling leaves of the Tree - which flourisheth in that City. With both his inner and his outer ear he will hear from its dust the hymns of glory and praise ascending unto the Lord of Lords, and with his inner eye will he discover the mysteries of "return" and "revival." How unspeakably glorious are the signs, the tokens, the revelations, and splendors which He Who is the King of names and attributes hath destined for that City! The attainment of this City quencheth thirst without water, and kindleth the love of God without fire. Within every blade of grass are enshrined the mysteries of an inscrutable wisdom, and upon every rose-bush a myriad nightingales pour out, in blissful rapture, their melody. Its wondrous tulips unfold the mystery of the undying Fire in the Burning Bush, and its sweet savors of holiness breathe the perfume of the Messianic Spirit. It bestoweth wealth without gold, and conferreth immortality without death. In every leaf ineffable delights are treasured, and within every chamber unnumbered mysteries lie hidden.

They that valiantly labor in quest of God's will, when once they have renounced all else but Him, will be so attached and wedded to that City that a moment's separation from it would to them be unthinkable. They will hearken unto infallible proofs from the Hyacinth of that assembly, and receive the surest testimonies from the beauty of its Rose and the melody of its Nightingale. Once in about a thousand years shall this City be renewed and re-adorned.

Wherefore, O my friend, it behooveth Us to exert the highest endeavor to attain unto that City, and, by the grace of God and His loving-kindness, rend asunder the "veils of glory"; so that, with inflexible steadfastness, we may sacrifice our drooping souls in the path of the New Beloved. We should with tearful eyes, fervently and repeatedly, implore Him to grant us the favor of that grace. That city is none other than the Word of God revealed in every age and dispensation. In the days of Moses it was the Pentateuch; in the days of Jesus the Gospel; in the days of Muhammad the Messenger of God the Qur'an; in this day the Bayán; and in the dispensation of Him Whom God will make manifest His own Book—the Book unto which all the Books of former Dispensations must needs be referred, the Book which standeth amongst them all transcendent and supreme. In these cities spiritual sustenance is bountifully provided, and incorruptible delights have been ordained. The food they bestow is the bread of heaven, and the Spirit they impart is God's imperishable blessing. Upon detached souls they bestow the gift of Unity, enrich the destitute, and offer the cup of knowledge unto them who wander in the wilderness of ignorance. All the guidance, the blessings, the learning, the understanding, the faith, and certitude, conferred upon all that is in heaven and on earth, are hidden and treasured within these Cities.

— *Bahá'u'lláh*

PERSPICUOUS VERSES

Blessed art thou, who hast fixed thy gaze upon Me, for this Tablet which hath been sent down for thee —a Tablet which causeth the souls of men to soar.
— Baha'u'llah

Among others, these perspicuous verses have, in answer to certain individuals, been sent down from the Kingdom of Divine knowledge:

O thou who hast set thy face towards the splendors of My Countenance! Vague fancies have encompassed the dwellers of the earth and debarred them from turning towards the Horizon of Certitude, and its brightness, and its manifestations and its lights. Vain imaginings have withheld them from Him Who is the Self-Subsisting. They speak as prompted by their own caprices, and understand not.

Among them are those who have said: "Have the verses been sent down?"

Say: "Yea, by Him Who is the Lord of the heavens!"

"Hath the Hour come?"

"Nay, more; it hath passed, by Him Who is the Revealer of clear tokens! Verily, the Inevitable is come, and He, the True One, hath appeared with proof and testimony. The Plain is disclosed, and mankind is sore vexed and fearful. Earthquakes have broken loose, and the tribes have lamented, for fear of God, the Lord of Strength, the All-Compelling."

Say: "The stunning trumpet-blast hath been loudly raised, and the Day is God's, the One, the Unconstrained."

"Hath the Catastrophe come to pass?"

Say: "Yea, by the Lord of Lords!"

"Is the Resurrection come?"

"Nay, more; He Who is the Self-Subsisting hath appeared with the Kingdom of His signs."

"Seest thou men laid low?"

"Yea, by my Lord, the Exalted, the Most High!"

"Have the tree-stumps been uprooted?"

"Yea, more; the mountains have been scattered in dust; by Him the Lord of attributes!"

They say: "Where is Paradise, and where is Hell?"

Say: "The one is reunion with Me; the other thine own self, O thou who dost associate a partner with God and doubtest."

They say: "We see not the Balance."

Say: "Surely, by my Lord, the God of Mercy! None can see it except such as are endued with insight."

"Have the stars fallen?"

Say: "Yea, when He Who is the Self-Subsisting dwelt in the Land of Mystery. Take heed, ye who are endued with discernment!" All the signs appeared when We drew forth the Hand of Power from the bosom of majesty and might. Verily, the Crier hath cried out, when the promised time came, and they that have recognized the splendors of Sinai have swooned away in the wilderness of hesitation, before the awful majesty of thy Lord, the Lord of creation.

The trumpet asketh: "Hath the Bugle been sounded?"

Say: "Yea, by the King of Revelation!, when He mounted the throne of His Name, the All-Merciful." Darkness hath been chased away by the dawning-light of the mercy of thy Lord, the Source of all light. The breeze of the All-Merciful hath wafted, and the souls have been quickened in the tombs of their bodies. Thus hath the decree been fulfilled by God, the Mighty, the Beneficent.

They that have gone astray have said: "When were the heavens cleft asunder?"

Say: "While ye lay in the graves of waywardness and error."

Among the heedless is he who rubbeth his eyes, and looketh to the right and to the left.

Say: "Blinded art thou. No refuge hast thou to flee to."

And among them is he who saith: "Have men been gathered together?"

Say: "Yea, by My Lord!, whilst thou didst lie in the cradle of idle fancies."

And among them is he who saith: "Hath the Book been sent down through the power of the true Faith?"

Say: "The true Faith itself is astounded. Fear ye, O ye men of understanding heart!"

And among them is he who saith: "Have I been assembled with others, blind?"

Say: "Yea, by Him that rideth upon the clouds!" Paradise is decked with mystic roses, and hell hath been made to blaze with the fire of the impious.

Say: "The light hath shone forth from the horizon of Revelation, and the whole earth hath been illumined at the coming of Him Who is the Lord of the Day of the Covenant!" The doubters have perished, whilst he that turned, guided by the light of assurance, unto the Dayspring of Certitude hath prospered.

Blessed art thou, who hast fixed thy gaze upon Me, for this Tablet which hath been sent down for thee—a Tablet which causeth the souls of men to soar. Commit it to memory, and recite it. By My life! It is a door to the mercy of thy Lord. Well is it with him that reciteth it at eventide and at dawn. We, verily, hear thy praise of this Cause, through which the mountain of knowledge was crushed, and men's feet have slipped. My glory be upon thee and upon whomsoever hath turned unto the Almighty, the All-Bounteous.

The Tablet is ended, but the theme is unexhausted. Be patient, for thy Lord is patient.

— *Bahá'u'lláh*

The Blessings

This is the final passage of the Most Holy Tablet (Lawḥ-i Aqdas), Bahá'u'lláh's Tablet to the Christians.

Blessed the slumberer who is awakened by My Breeze.

Blessed the lifeless one who is quickened through My reviving breaths.

Blessed the eye that is solaced by gazing at My beauty.

Blessed the wayfarer who directeth his steps towards the Tabernacle of My glory and majesty.

Blessed the distressed one who seeketh refuge beneath the shadow of My canopy.

Blessed the sore athirst who hasteneth to the soft-flowing waters of My loving-kindness.

Blessed the insatiate soul who casteth away his selfish desires for love of Me and taketh his place at the banquet table which I have sent down from the heaven of divine bounty for My chosen ones.

Blessed the abased one who layeth fast hold on the cord of My glory; and the needy one who entereth beneath the shadow of the Tabernacle of My wealth.

Blessed the ignorant one who seeketh the fountain of My knowledge; and the heedless one who cleaveth to the cord of My remembrance.

Blessed the soul that hath been raised to life through My quickening breath and hath gained admittance into My heavenly Kingdom.

Blessed the man whom the sweet savors of reunion with Me have stirred and caused to draw nigh unto the Dayspring of My Revelation.

Blessed the ear that hath heard and the tongue that hath borne witness and the eye that hath seen and recognized the Lord

Himself, in His great glory and majesty, invested with grandeur and dominion.

Blessed are they that have attained His presence.

Blessed the man who hath sought enlightenment from the Day-Star of My Word.

Blessed he who hath attired his head with the diadem of My love.

Blessed is he who hath heard of My grief and hath arisen to aid Me among My people.

Blessed is he who hath laid down his life in My path and hath borne manifold hardships for the sake of My Name.

Blessed the man who, assured of My Word, hath arisen from among the dead to celebrate My praise.

Blessed is he that hath been enraptured by My wondrous melodies and hath rent the veils asunder through the potency of My might.

Blessed is he who hath remained faithful to My Covenant, and whom the things of the world have not kept back from attaining My Court of holiness.

Blessed is the man who hath detached himself from all else but Me, hath soared in the atmosphere of My love, hath gained admittance into My Kingdom, gazed upon My realms of glory, quaffed the living waters of My bounty, hath drunk his fill from the heavenly river of My loving providence, acquainted himself with My Cause, apprehended that which I concealed within the treasury of My Words, and hath shone forth from the horizon of divine knowledge engaged in My praise and glorification. Verily, he is of Me. Upon him rest My mercy, My loving-kindness, My bounty and My glory.

—*Bahá'u'lláh*